Invading God's Space

Longing for His Presence

R.M. Coleman

First edition
This book was professionally typeset on Reedsy. Find out more at reedsy.com

Introduction

God Invaders

Throughout time, there have always been "God invaders." The Bible and church history are full of them. You had everyone from Abraham and Moses, who had face-to-face encounters with God, to David, the righteous king who worshipped out of his priestly garments and established 24/7 open worship just to be in the Lord's presence. Then, you had William Seymour of the Azusa Street Revival, who wore a box over his head until God spoke to him in one of the greatest revivals that Los Angeles California has ever witnessed, transforming lives and crossing racial lines in 1906. These are just a few of the countless God invaders.

Today, there's an underground movement happening all around us. God invaders are those who don't sit back and wait on God to come down to them—they're the ones who pry open the heavens and invade God's space. They're not too concerned about the religious protocol and rites. They pursue the tangible presence of God. God invaders can't stand a dead, stale church service. They're not after yesteryear presences of God; they want a fresh, new encounter with Him each and every time they worship Him. There's no stopping a God invader when they want to apprehend the one who they're longing for.

Disappointingly, in today's church, we don't have too many God invaders. We're so stuck on wondering what God has done and what He's about to do. Few people can say, "*I* have Him and *this* is what He's doing right now." We get excited about His Word and a prophetic word. But how excited would you be if you could open up the heavens and invade God's space? *Are* you ready to invade God's space?

Are you ready to open up the heavens and tell God, "Tag! You're it!"? Let's get ready to invade God's space together.

1

A Place Called the Watchers: The Outer Court

In the ancient times of Israel, the temple was the focal point of the nation and of worship. It is said to have been built with splendor and beauty. The craftsmanship would have the architects of today in awe, just like the ancient people of that day whenever they came into Jerusalem to celebrate the feast days. If you would allow me, I will take you on a tour of the different places of worship that we must go through to mature into the bride of Christ.

I want to use Herod's Temple as an example to offer prophetic insights into how we should grow into intimacy with God. The first place we will start is at the outer court. This is the place where money was being exchanged and sacrifices were being bought. This is also the famous place where Jesus cleansed the temple by flipping over the money exchange tables. There are two types of people in this area of the temple. You have those who I call the "watchers" and the "surrenders."

The watchers are those who have not yet made a full commitment to becoming surrenderers. These are the people who will watch you praise and worship your way into God's presence, obtaining his blessings by baptism of the Holy Spirit, laying on of hands, or by prophetic word. They will watch with criticism, saying:

"It doesn't take all of that."

"God's not in that."

"Why are they dancing like that?"

"Don't they know that they will get dirty by lying at the altar?"

"Somebody should tell them to stop shouting so loud."

They will even complain about how the pastor or guest speaker should have preached the Word of God. We see these same watchers in the Book of Exodus, where God told Moses to set up the tent of meetings outside of the camp. That was to be the place where He would meet all of Israel or those who sought Him.

Before I move further, I want to stop right here and look at that word "sought." In the Hebrew tongue, it is the word "baqash" (baw-kash'), which means to "set about," "looking," and "a search will be made." Can I just say it in a prophetic way what sought means to me? To me, it means, "opening up blinded eyes."

When the pillar of cloud came down from heaven in front of the doorway of the tabernacle, Moses and Joshua went into the tent before the Lord. The Lord spoke to Moses with instructions, directions and revelation. Every time Moses spoke with God, his eyes were opened a little more. But the watchers of the camp stood at the entranceway of their tents and watched Moses and Joshua get blessed by the Lord.

The watchers will never understand that, by them getting into the presence of the Lord, He can open up their eyes more to get them out of their circumstances. They don't understand that, by getting into God's presence, He could bring them peace. They don't know that getting into God's presence will increase their faith.

I think you're getting a clear picture of the watchers in your local church. You know the ones who will complain about everything, but will never do anything. They may be *in* the church, but the world is in *them*. The outer court is a place of decision: the place where you will decide whether you will surrender or stay in the world. In ancient times, this was a place that was prepared for those who no longer wanted to be a part of the world; they were ready to repent. This was the place where the priest blew the silver trumpets before one could enter through the gates with thanksgiving.

There's not too much to say about the surrenders because that's just what they did: *surrendered!* These are the people who have given up what was once valuable to them, just for the opportunity to walk through the gates with thanksgiving and be forgiven. But, in order to become a surrender, there's a starting point. We all have and need to start at our outer court experience, which is the place of Jabbok.

2

A Place Called the Surrenders: Jabbok

Jabbok is a river that is highlighted in the Book of Genesis. Something great happened there. Jabbok has a special meaning to you and to Jacob. It means "a place of passing over"; it can also mean "struggle, to empty and pour out." Jabbok is the place where Jacob struggled or wrestled with an angel. This is the place where Jacob received the new name of "Israel" and a new character. It's where he totally surrendered to God. So, the outer court is our version of Jabbok.

Jabbok is a lonely place. Your mother can't help you. Your pastor can't help you. Your spouse can't help. No one can help you. This is where you face God face to face to allow Him to drive out the Jacob that's in you.

If we were to tell the truth, most of us still have some Jacob in us. We're deceitful, dishonest—one who cheats his brother or sister. There can be no victories in our lives if we don't deal with the reality of ourselves at the brook of Jabbok. The majority of us are religiously mature, but spiritually immature. See, Jacob had a religious experience like all of us once we rested at Bethel (the house of God). Sunday after Sunday, the outer court folks, or the watchers, only come to church to get a *religious* experience. They dance, shout and speak in other tongues. They get excited about the material promises of God and stop there; that's as far as they will go with God.

Listen. A religious experience will *never* change your character. Only a face-to-face encounter with God will. An experience has an expiration date on it, while an *encounter* will leave you, like Jacob, with a limp for a lifetime. It's sad to say that many in the body of Christ are living off an expired experience! In my household, we call that "spoiled." If the milk is a day past its expiration date, I'm not drinking it. I'll pour it out and go get a fresh gallon with a new expiration date.

Now Bethel (the house of God) is not a bad place. We should desire to have fresh, new experiences with God. But we tend to get stuck there and create idols based off those experiences. We try to sing the same songs to recapture that moment from the week before, and it never happens. Why is that? It is because God has said, *"Behold, I make all things new"* (Revelation 21:5, KJV). So, if God makes all things new, His heart's desire is for His children to experience Him in a new way.

Jabbok is a place for us to empty ourselves *of* ourselves. This occurs when we have made up in our minds that we are no longer going to be watchers—experiencing the supernatural presence of God, yet never dealing with the Jacob within us—and become committed to giving up our lives and picking up our cross to follow Jesus. Now, for the rest of us who want to move on to the next place in intimacy with God, let's walk through the gates with thanksgiving.

3

A Place Called the Absolute Surrenders: The Inner Court

The next level that we enter is the inner court. I call this a place of absolute surrender. The first thing you would encounter when entering the inner court was the brazen altar. This is where one would present their animal offering or sacrifice to the priests, who would make atonement and intercession. Prophetically, the brazen altar represents man's sinfulness, where our sins and flesh must be slaughtered so that we can begin to look like Christ. This is the place where we start living a life of repentance and giving up our bodies as a living sacrifice unto God.

The next thing you would see is the laver, or basin, filled with water to wash hands and feet. The word "laver" means "bathe or wash all over." The Apostle Paul stated something similar in the Book of Ephesians: *"to make her holy, cleansing her by the washing with water through the word"* (Ephesians 5:26, KJV). Positioned between the door of the Holy Place and the brazen altar, the great purpose of the laver was for the priests to wash and cleanse themselves from defilement before they entered the Holy Place and after they left.

Absolute surrender and repentance always come before serving God. The washing of the hands deals with service and work. The hands of the priest had to be cleansed daily, but the initial cleansing was done once. The initial cleansing is symbolic of Jesus dying for us once and for all: that He cleansed us of all unrighteousness and has made us righteous because of His blood. But we still need a daily cleansing of our hands by repenting before we serve and do the work of God.

The washing of the feet deals with your way of life. The priest's walk had to be a different kind of walk—it had to be a holy walk. So, their feet had to always be cleansed. We all know the story of Jacob, where he struggled with the angel and the angel touched his hip, causing it to dislocate. When Jacob got up from the ground, he had a limp. But not just any limp—it was a *holy limp*. I'm sorry, but I can't trust anyone who hasn't been touched by God and who doesn't have a holy limp!

If you can't prevail in your struggle with God, then you have no victory. That word "prevail" means "to gain the upper hand, to gain the victory, to gain superiority." You can only prevail when God has accepted your commitment to surrender to His will for your life.

A Place Called Revelation: The Holy Place

Now that we have moved to the next stage of our intimacy with the Father, let's go inside the Holy Place. When coming into the Holy Place, you would see the table of showbread to your right. Then, you would also see the menorah lit and the golden altar of incense. Everyone was not allowed into this sacred place; only the priest. I want us to take our attention to the table of showbread. The showbread was literally called "bread of the presence (of God)." In Hebrew, it is known as the "bread of faces," with twelve loaves of wheat bread corresponding to the twelve tribes of Israel.

The bread of faces is the face and presence of Jesus: the bread of life that came down from heaven and revealed Himself to humanity (John 6:35, 51). In John 8:12 (KJV), Jesus says, *"I am the bread of life: He that cometh to me shall never hunger; and he that believeth on me shall never thirst,"* and *"I am the living bread which came down from heaven: If any man eat of this bread, he shall live forever: and the bread that I will give is my flesh, which I will give for the life of the world."*

The Holy Place is where Jesus reveals Himself continually and releases mysteries of the kingdom of heaven. The Bible tells us that after the resurrection, Jesus revealed Himself to Mary and the disciples, along with others, for forty days. The Apostle Paul tells us that he received mysteries from Jesus (Galatians 1:12). Not only is this a place of revelation of Jesus and mysteries of the kingdom of God, but it's also the source of all light. The menorah was made of solid gold and weighed 75 pounds. Gold represented the presences of God and His holiness, while everything outside in the courtyard was made of bronze.

The golden lampstand foreshadowed Jesus' coming because the menorah was the only source of light in the Holy Place; windows were not built into that room. Jesus also compares us to light in Matthew 5:14, 16 (KJV): *"Ye are the light of the world. A city that is set on a hill cannot be hid...Let your light so shine before men, that they may see your good works, and glorify your Father which is in heaven."*

The lampstand had six branches that resembled the branches of an almond tree. There was a reason why God created this resemblance. Now the word "almond" in Hebrew has the root word "shaked," meaning to "watch," "wait" and "hasten." In other terms, it was God saying that He will watch and bring His promises to pass.

In Jeremiah 1:11 (KJV), the prophet says, *"Moreover the word of the Lord came unto me, saying, 'Jeremiah, what seest thou?' And I said, 'I see a rod of an almond tree.' Then said the Lord unto me, 'thou hast well seen: for I will hasten my word to perform it.'"* Jesus is the lampstand and the almond tree. He releases revelation to us by saying, "I am the light of the world" and "watches over his promises."

The Holy Place is also a place of divine visitation where you receive understanding of what God is calling you to do for His kingdom. Here, God gives assurance, confidence and instructions in the hearts of His people to fulfill their calling. The Holy Place is an awesome place for those who reach this stage of intimacy. They love this place in God so that, at times, people tend to settle down here and call it home. It can be a very difficult time leaving.

The Holy Place is a mountaintop type of experience because God gives you room to grow and develop an understanding in your destiny, prayer, relationship, revelation and His visitations. Here, you learn how to walk with God among other followers of Christ. He uses the Holy Place to strengthen and deepen your intimacy and fellowship with Him. God truly longs to have fellowship and intimacy with His people, and the Holy Place is the place that will help us do just that.

A Place Called the Seekers: The Holy of Holies

We come now to the Holy of Holies. This was a fairly small room separated from the Holy Place. The Ark of the Covenant was the only piece of furniture, and only the light from God lit up the room. We know this as His "Shekinah," the glory of the Lord. When entering the Holy of Holies, you would notice something very quickly: there was no seat. There was only one seat reserved, and that was the mercy seat of God. When the high priest would enter once a year, he would enter with his head bowed low, barefoot with bells all around his robe.

This is a place for those who *really* seek God! Jeremiah 29:13 (KJV) says, *"You will seek me and find me when you search for me with all your heart."* Seekers are those who will not stop searching for God's glory. They think, dream, drink, write, breathe and speak of His majesty. The greatest seeker of them all, in my opinion, was King David. God stated that David was after His own heart, and God felt strongly about David chasing after His presence. Before David was king, he was a shepherd boy, worshipping and speaking to God in the plains while leading and protecting his sheep. He made God king of his heart. Before God crowns you in your life, you must crown Him first of your life.

In these last days, the true seekers will be called prophetically David's Tabernacle. If we interpret what David did to return the Ark of the Covenant to Jerusalem prophetically, it's the same blueprint we should use to return the presence of God to the church. David longed to see God manifest between the two cherubim wings because he knew that God's presence represented power, healing, victory, favor, blessings, and most of all, intimacy. Seekers seek after God's face, not his hand, because seeking God's hand doesn't bring intimacy—it brings blessings. But seekers know that God's intimacy trumps blessings. When you have God's attention, you have everything you need.

When you read the account of David bringing back the Ark of the Covenant to Jerusalem with dance and worship, his actions irritated and embarrassed Michal, his wife. Likewise, your identity as a seeker can sometimes become embarrassing and irritating to the Michals in your life. It shows that a seeker values the things God values.

Michal chose her dignity over God's deity. For that reason, she became barren, for David ceased intimacy with her and she died without having any children. Dignitaries and religious rulers will keep a church barren. There will be no new fruit, no new anointing, no new moves of God, no new growth, no revelation released, no new visions, no new dreams, no knowledge, no understanding, no move of the prophetic, no moves in gifts—everything is dead!

When worship is veiled for a seeker, it hinders their ability to see the glory of God they are pursuing. This only happens in a dry and barren church that still sings the same old songs from yesteryear. The choir is singing the songs dead, dry and sad, just like the old musty choir robes that they wear. If you are in a ministry like this, you need to run as far away from it as possible. God wants to give us new and fresh songs—fresh moves of His Spirit, without any limitation. We just need to be open to the rhema moves of God and ride the current rivers of Holy Spirit to be revived.

The tabernacle of David was different from the tabernacle of Moses and the temple of Solomon. What Moses and Solomon built hid the glory of God from the people's sight. Whereas, with the tabernacle of David, everyone from far and near, from believers to strangers, saw God's glory. Having a seeker's relationship with God will cause everyone to see His glory upon you, like the face of Moses when he came down from the presence of God from the mountain.

6

A Place Called the Lovers' Lane: Bedchamber

You have to be special or important to be summoned into the bedchamber of the king. The bedchamber, better known as the bride chamber, is the ultimate place that every believer wants to be. This is where God shares things with you that He doesn't share with just any of His children. Now God is no respecter of person, but He *can* choose favorites. When you have the heart of God, you have access and influence in His kingdom.

In my house, I have a sitting room where I do a lot of reading and unwinding after a long day. At times, my wife will come and sit with me. I really get excited when she comes into the room because I know that she's going to start an intimate conversation. That usually will lead me, one way or another, out of the house to get her something that she's requesting of me.

I would do anything for my bride, at any time. However, it's even better when she comes to spend time with me. I love when she comes to sit right under me just to talk. I love those moments the most because it reminds me of what the Father desires from us. He too longs to have those moments with us, where we just sit up under Him and talk to Him. Those moments when we're not asking for anything; we're just loving on Him. So, at the end of every conversation I have with my wife, I say, "What do you want?"

Can you even imagine that, after your intimate encounter with the Father, He'll say, "What is it that you want?" This is what's going on in the bride chamber. You have to be a lover of God to enter into this realm! God says in Proverbs 8:17 (KJV): *"I love them that love me; and those who seek me early shall find me."* God gets excited over you when you want to spend time with Him. There are things He wants to show you and tell you.

7

The Day I Drew Near

On November 13, 2011, at 4:20 a.m., I woke up out of a dream. I felt this weightiness in my stomach. Revelation 10:10 says, *And I took the little book out of the angel's hand, and ate it, and in mouth sweet as honey and as soon as I had eaten it, my belly was bitter.* (KJV) So, I went into my computer room, where most of my time is spent, and made it into my prayer room. As I began to pray, the Holy Spirit told me that God saw what I was doing. He saw what I was going through, and He cared about me.

Then, the Holy Spirit said to me, "Seek His face, Rahsaan. Seek His face. You have to seek His face. You have to seek His face. I see what you're going through, but you have to seek His face." From that day, I understood that if I draw near to God, he will draw near to me.

Many of us think that we know who God is and what God is like. Many of us have even gone to school to acquire a piece of paper that shows we've completed our "God" courses I, too, thought I needed to do the same thing. And yet, many of us still never take the time to *truly know* Him.

I'll never forget the day that I heard God's voice while in that class. "Leave this place and I'll teach you," He said. Every day after that moment, I read the Bible for hours. The words were coming off of the pages. I gained more understanding of the Scriptures. It was a fantastic feeling. That is, until I came across this Scripture: *But ye have received the Spirit of adoption, whereby we cry, Abba, Father* (Romans 8:15, KJV).

As I sat at my computer desk in awe, I said, "You want me to call you 'Daddy'?"

Immediately, God replied with a soft voice, saying, "Yes. You are my son and I am your Father."

I cried tears of joy. I felt something falling off of me. Since that moment, I can't wait to draw near to Him. James 4:8 says, *Draw near to God, and He will draw near to you* (KJV). In Matthew, there's a story about a woman who drew near to God. It forever changed her life.

Now when Jesus was in Bethany, in the house of Simon the leper, there came unto him a woman having an alabaster box of very precious ointment, and poured it on his head, as he sat at meat (Matthew 26:6-7, KJV). This woman came out of nowhere and interrupted Jesus' leadership luncheon. What boldness she had to approach the King of kings and willingly pour out upon Him some expensive ointment, while He was getting ready to bless the food.

When drawing close to God, you're going to have to give up something that is valuable to you. The young, rich ruler wanted to draw near to Jesus, until Jesus told him to sell all that he owned (Matthew 19:16-22, KJV). He couldn't part ways with the things he placed great value on. What are you willing to give up for God? What are you willing to do? Can you honestly say, "God, I don't want any of this. I just want you!"? Now, drawing near to God doesn't make you a super Christian. It makes you a willing vessel, the kind of Christian who does whatever it takes to get to God.

When drawing close to God, you will do some things that will look embarrassing to others. It will be in the process of worshipping Him. The woman with the alabaster box wiped her tears from Jesus' feet with her hair while applying kisses in between each wipe. Now that's pure worship! Do you know what would happen if saints across the body of Christ were to corporately worship God in this manner? A lot of idols in our lives that we hold great value toward would be ruined.

When drawing close to God, He will cast away everything that's not like Him from your life. He will ruin your little church programs that you worked on for months. He will ruin those plans that you have for your life that He never planned for you. He will ruin that horrible marriage that you're in and make it a Garden of Eden. My prayer is that God will ruin everything in our lives that stands in between us and Him.

8

Got Hunger?

One of the main ingredients to drawing close to God is hunger! The woman with the alabaster box had a divine hunger for Jesus. She was tired of the same religious system that was cheating the people out of a true experience with the true and living God. The Pharisees of that day only wanted offerings in exchange for an illusion of God's presence. She wasn't embarrassed; she was embracing her divine hunger. When you no longer want to eat what is being preached to you because you're tired of the same leftovers again and again, that's when divine hunger will set in.

The woman pushed aside all of her pride and allowed her hunger to do all of the talking for her. When your divine hunger taps God on His shoulder, He will turn around and satisfy it. For He says in Matthew 5:6 (KJV), *"Blessed are those who hunger and thirst for righteousness, for they will be filled."* With every fiber within her soul and heart, she passionately pursued Him.

When you're chasing after God, no one and nothing matters. The reason that the people around you can't understand your radical love and worship for God is because they don't have the appetite that you do. They're not ravenously hungry like you are. When you get to this level of hunger for God, all of your good manners go out of the window. Have you ever seen a person so hungry that their face is literally in the plate, and you never see them chew the food that they're eating? This was the woman with the alabaster box. She didn't care about Simon, the leper. She didn't care about Judas and what he was saying about her, and she most definitely didn't care about the rest of the disciples, who were watching as she poured out her expensive worship upon Jesus.

The problem here is that we have lost our hunger for God. We have allowed earthly things to temporarily satisfy our cravings and sustain our lives. Week after week, month after month, year after year, we attend church services just to fill a void in our lives for that moment. But we're never fully satisfied by the one who is causing the hunger placed in our spirits. Not only that, but we tend to allow what others are going to say influence our actions when we are led to worship God in uncommon ways. At times, the Holy Spirit will tell you to kneel down, lift up your hands or even shout. But, we are afraid of the Judases who tell us that we could have used that type of worship for something else. At times in our lives, we have to be like blind Bartimaeus. We have to do whatever it takes to get God's attention, no matter who tries to shut us up or stop us!

9

I'm Desperate for You

In our society, everyone wants more: more money, more time, more home, more car, and let's not forget more food. Listen, if we put down our church programs and see that God has more to offer us, and that He wants us to want Him more, then we can live in a place of abundance in Him. Bartimaeus is a great prophetic picture of mankind. The name Bartimaeus means "unclean son." But he's the son of Timaeus, which means "highly prized/honor." Even though we were unclean sons of Yahweh, we were still His highly prized sons of honor. And that's why He sent Jesus to save us.

Now, Bartimaeus was desperate for something to happen when he heard that Jesus was walking by. The sound of desperation is a much higher frequency than the norm. When someone is in desperate need of something, they're brutally honest. They will cause you to stop in your tracks with their attempts to get your attention. Desperation has a tendency to humble us. But, at the same time, it can make us bold—to the point that our desperation causes a distraction around us. Do you think Bartimaeus cared if those around him were getting frustrated with him yelling out to Jesus in his desperation? He didn't care if his cries would cause offense to anyone. Bartimaeus was showing Jesus that his very survival depended on His ability to heal him.

This high frequency of desperation will cause others to feel uncomfortable and awkward. Bartimaeus was disturbing the comfort zone of others, who should have been crying out along with him. They knew who Jesus was. They heard what Jesus had done, and yet they were trying to get Bartimaeus to shut up and stop his blessing. Scripture tells us that the only ones who were blind were the ones who were trying to stop Bartimaeus from getting into the presence of Jesus. Those are the watchers I've spoken about! I guess they didn't have any issues or problems because they surely didn't have enough compassion for Bartimaeus to take him by the hand and walk him over to Jesus.

Right now, there's a growing sense of hunger and desperation in our churches—a deep conviction of, "There has to be more than this!" We want to stumble, kneel and lie flat on our faces in the glory of God. If we don't leave room for hunger and desperation in our services, though, we're just showing up to empty buildings, singing empty songs, and listening to empty sermons when God wants us to be filled to overflow!

10

Hunger Games

I loved *The Hunger Games* movie. I wasn't really interested in it until my wife asked me to watch it with her one day. I was so drawn in to the storyline that I had to watch the four parts, too—I had to know how it would end.

If you've never seen the movies, or read the original novels before, it's about these kids getting thrown into survival tournaments out in the wilderness. It's kill or be killed. And I got to thinking: *At times, God will play "hunger games" with us.* God will cause a famine to come into our lives, which will make us go into a survival mode. It stirs up hunger in us for more of Him. The Book of Ruth opens by saying, *Now it came to pass in the days when the judges ruled, that there was a famine in the land* (KJV). The story further says that Elimelech left Bethlehem-Judah and led his entire family into the land of Moab. While in the process of settling there, he and his two sons died.

The name Elimelech means, "My God is King." Bethlehem-Judah means, "House/place of bread in the City of Praise." Moab means, "Who's your father?" We have to be very careful where we lead our families when the Word of the Lord has dried up in the place at which we worship. What I'm saying is not an excuse for church-hopping, though there are points in our lives where the Lord will lead us out of a ministry so that we can grow.

If the Lord plants us in a ministry, He can pluck us up and plant us in a bigger place. If you are a green thumb, you will totally understand what I'm about to describe. Any time that you have a plant, and it outgrows the pottery, you have to dig it out and place it into a bigger flower pot for it to maximize its growth in its new place. Again, it's the same with us. We can only go and grow as far as the person that is leading and feeding us, which leads me to the next point. Elimelech made an emotional decision when the famine came and his survival mode kicked in.

How does one that goes by the name "My God is King" leave the House of Bread in the City of Praise for a land where he doesn't know who his father is? Moab was a land of idolatry—

a land that had many gods. One of the gods that they serviced was Moloch. Now, Moloch was an idol god that had a human form with a bull's head. Its hands were stretched out to receive the children for human sacrifice or the passing through the fire, as Scripture states. This big move happened because Naomi, Elimelech's wife, heard a rumor that God was blessing the people with fresh bread in that land. In the times of famine, bread becomes sacred.

We, as the church, tend to advertise that, "God is over here! Come and get a real word of the Lord!" Many of us are leaving the house of bread and going into these ministries on a rumor that God is blessing the people. When we show up, we don't see nor smell fresh bread baking. Instead, we only see and smell the flesh of man's entertainment. This reminds me of what the Pharisees did in the Old Testament. They were focused on entertaining the people so that their big secret wouldn't get out: that God was no longer manifesting His glory behind the veil. And He hasn't been behind that veil for a very long time.

In the last book of the Old Testament, the Prophet Malachi spoke to the leaders under the command of the Lord, who ministered to the Lord, accusing them of robbing Him. The leaders played dumb because they weren't going to stop robbing God. So, God stopped speaking for 400 years. He stopped manifesting Himself in the Holy of Holies. Can you imagine that the leaders kept up with the religious rites, knowing that God had stopped approving the offerings that the people were giving? God even stopped talking to his prophets until His plan was coming into place.

John stepped on the scene dressed like the Prophet Elijah, and the Pharisees were worried because they thought the Day of the Lord was upon them. For the Scripture says that, *"The Lord will send Elijah first before the great and terrible day of the Lord"* (Joel 2:31). And when it came to Jesus, the Pharisees were worried that they would lose the people and the money that they were making by selling blemished animals for false sacrifices, not knowing that Jesus was the manifested presence of God wrapped in flesh. The Pharisees prophetically represent those religious spirits that like to block the knowledge of God, stop the flow of the Holy Spirit, and preserve the things of the past, like where God has been and what God has done. Jesus prophetically represents the past, present and future. He represents where God has been, where God is now, and where God is going to be.

There's a new generation of God's people who are dissatisfied with the status quo of the religious rituals and traditions of men. These are the people who have a hunger for God that can't be quenched by all the circuses, parlor tricks and acts. They're like the woman with the alabaster box, bypassing all the religious protocols and upsetting every religious ceremony. But no earthly person can quench this holy passion for the presence of God. It's very hurtful to see this spirit of entertainment running rampant in the church, let alone seeing it being welcomed with opened arms. The generals of faith who were full of Holy Spirit wouldn't allow this spirit to enter their places of worship. We are no longer worshipping God, but worshipping these ministers and their newfound deep revelation. Worship has been replaced with performance, and these performers have caused our worshippers to stop worshipping God and become spectators.

The early church fathers had a sense of reverence toward God that brought them into His presence. They were totally captivated and in awed silence before the presence of God. Sadly, in an exciting way, we are seeing the prophetic words of Paul and Jude coming to pass, when they stated that men have crept in unawares teaching false doctrine and telling fables (Jude 1:4; 2 Timothy 4:4). This is causing this generation's church to become spiritually impotent. God's presence has lost its priority in today's church. There are those who feed the people of God with old, molded bread from yesteryear. I'm not sure if we would even recognize the presence of God if He entered our place of worship.

Some of us have to learn how to be desperately grateful for what God has done and what He is presently doing. We also have to be desperately hungry for him. When a baby is hungry, he or she will wake up the whole house crying out to eat. You can be in a good, deep sleep, and that baby can wake you right up with its cries of hunger. Most of us have awakened from our religious sleep, and now we're hungry. And because of this hunger for God, we should be loud enough to wake everyone up from their religious slumbers, too. That's what religion will do to you: put you to sleep spiritually and numb your sense of God's presence.

Most of us are good with just going to church and hearing a great word to feed our flesh, but not our spirit man. We still leave spiritually hungry. I am fed up with man's traditions and activities, all in the name of the Lord. I pray that people will wake up and find out that God has much more to offer. Until God's people get hungry for the true presence of God, and invade His space, we will be feeding our flesh with stale crumbs of man's bread instead of the bread of life.

One reason why most people "church-hop" is because their spirit is calling out to the depths of God. If they're sensitive enough to recognize this divine calling from God to seek Him, and not a church, prophet or pastor, but Him alone. Then, and only then, can they find what's been ailing them. God has a calendar, and He has scheduled an appointment for His divine encounter to meet you. I feel a divine dryness that's causing a divine hunger for a divine encounter with God's divine presence. Are you hungry enough to meet Him?

11

We're Out of Fresh Bread

There's so much in and to God that we haven't tapped into as a body as a whole that we're doing a disservice to the lost and to ourselves. Week in and week out, we gather in our services to eat bread that has become stale and molded. Leaders are trying to duplicate yesteryear's movements, without asking God what He's doing in this "right-now" moment. We're content and satisfied with what is given to us. We never take the necessary time to really press into the presence of God to obtain the fresh bread He has baked for us. Will anyone be bold enough to walk into the kitchen of God and shout, "We're out of fresh bread!"?

I have a favorite restaurant that my wife and I love frequent. They have the best butter cheddar cheese bread in the business. Just thinking of that fresh, hot bread makes me hungry. Well, the waiter will bring the bread to us in a basket--hot, soft and fresh. Once we eat the whole basket of bread, we get the attention of the waiter and let them know we've run out. They get right on it by heading back to the kitchen to bring us more.

Likewise, God has prepared hot, soft, fresh bread for us in abundance, but the waiters and waitresses are ignoring the people who they're supposed to serve. We have millions inside and outside the church who're hungry for the bread of life, the bread of God, the showbread. Everyone has become spiritual coaches, self-help gurus or self-advancement counselors. No one sees the sign in God's window saying, "Help wanted—looking for servers."

Who can blame the people for leaving the church? If I were in an establishment and the service was poor, I'd get up and leave, as well. But now, we have the people turning to these Christian psychics, astrologists and spiritualists, who disguise themselves as prophets for fresh bread and direction. This world is spiritually hungry for God, but no one wants to be the carriers of His hot, fresh bread. Thus, the counterfeits are welcomed and accepted as the authentic. If we would take off our costumes of purple and scarlet, and our big hats and robes…if we would stop hiding our insecurities behind these things and become who God has called us to be…if we would simply tell Him that we're out of fresh bread to feed the poor in spirit, then the world would see Jesus through us. There's a story in Mark 6:41 of a little boy who had a basket, which contained two fish and five loaves of bread. This young boy didn't know that God was using him as a waiter on one of the greatest days to see a miracle. The disciples asked Jesus, "How are we going to feed this crowd?" One of the disciples brought the little boy over to Jesus. At that moment, Jesus took the basket and fed the whole crowd fresh, hot bread and fish.

God wants to restore fresh bread to the church so we can once again experience true revival! At this point of my life, I'm tired of hearing of yesteryear revival because I'm hungry for a right-now revival! We have fallen into a dangerous place where we're telling others to come to our man-made, two- and three-day revivals. This only benefits church members in the sense of keeping them engaged with the stale, boring and dead church *and church programs*. True revival only comes from true hunger, truly waiting on the Lord, and true repentance. Right now, all we're doing is having conversations outside of God's kitchen and pretending that we're working as servers.

A Weakened State

If we're truly honest with ourselves concerning the condition of the church in America, and around the world, we know that she's on the brink of the great falling away. We're dealing with some serious threats. With how the church stands now, it will be no surprise when the day comes that our churches will be left empty and desolate. There's no difference between the holy and profane, godliness and worldliness. The Bible has no compromises. Yet, we have given up our responsibilities as the Church for comfort and motivational speakers, who are leading our churches. We're on a sinking ship, and it seems like the band is still playing. But Yahweh has a message. That message is to wake up the church and come back to Him!

I believe we're living in a right-now generation that's breaking free from the bondage of religion and the traditions of men. We're beginning to seek the face of God and get back to the origin of things. The generals of faith who established the foundation of the church say, in Proverbs 22:28, *Remember not the ancient landmarks, which thy fathers have set* (KJV). The landmarks have been removed by men who believed that we should cover up the old wells that were dug up.

In the time of ancient Israel, there was a generation that rose up and got rid of the traditions of men and the religious hula hoops. At this time, Israel moved away from what was established and began to pursue other gods, while disregarding the prophets who came to warn them of pending judgments. Israel began to adapt to the other nations' cultures, and the lines between them blurred.

You couldn't tell Israel from the other nations. Israel had a right-now generation that had grown tired of the religious parlor tricks and circus shows. They'd come across the true Word of God. It pricked their hearts so that it moved them to destroy anything and everything that looked like religion from the previous generation. In today's terms, we would call this a "revival" or an "awakening." This was done by the King of Israel, Josiah. At this time, he was only eight years of age. His actions led to a reformed Israel (2 Kings 22-23). This right-now generation sees through the deception and those who are corrupt in our churches. We're looking for something that's real and that has substance.

In 2 Timothy 3:5, the Apostle Paul tells us, ...*a form of godliness, but denying the power thereof, from such turn away* (KJV). There comes a time when a dissatisfied generation rises up. It's because they're hungry for God and they're tired of the status quo. This holy hunger can't be quenched by a man-made revival. They want to bypass all of the religious protocols and rituals, and get straight to the presence of God.

Most of our leaders in our churches today have the spirit of the Pharisees. They want to control, condemn and put those who have a true hunger and passion for God out of the church. But here's the sad part: They're kicking out *the church*. So, you have these leaders who are willing to put the church of God out of the church of men. More than anything, the church of God should be *welcome* in the churches of men! Can't we see the grave danger that we're in? Can't anyone see the spirit of Babylon running rampant—not only in the churches of America—but all over the globe? There are three clear signs to recognize the spirit of Babylon in the church. You have the spirit of shiftlessness, the spirit of comfort, and the spirit of performance/entertainment. Let me describe these spirits that are working under the war chief, the spirit of Babylon.

The Spirit of Shiftlessness

We can say the church has become lethargic, or, in better terms, has become lazy. We have a lack of energy and enthusiasm. We're so stuck on yesteryear's triumphs that we never move forward or move the Kingdom of God. It's okay to thank God for our past victories, but we have greater victories that still need to be won! We're just sitting back, settled in our churches and waiting on God to move, when God is waiting on *us* to get off our butts and move forward. We can't preach the gospel only within those four walls and think that the lost will come to our services. We must get out of the church and *become* the church that the world needs to see. Jesus was never lazy when it came to showing the love of the Father or sharing the gospel. The church is really a place for teaching and development for people to be launched out into the world.

The Spirit of Comfort

Some have this idea that the struggle of the church is over, while others believe that their generation is going to heaven. One thing that sticks out for me is that many have no expectations. Most of the church has grown stagnant and succumbed to the spirit of comfort. They would rather sit back and wait on the by-and-by, not wanting to be disturbed while they enjoy their religion. Wake up, church! Let's flow again with the power of Holy Spirit. The earlier church paid a heavy price for their faith in Christ. They didn't sit back and enjoy their religion. As a matter of fact, they *hated* anything that dealt with religion. They were never at ease when they lived and preached the gospel. Jesus said to the disciples in Acts 1:8, *"But ye shall receive power, after that the Holy Spirit is come upon you: and ye shall become my witnesses unto me both in Jerusalem, and in Judaea, and in Samaria, and unto the uttermost part of the earth"* (KJV). The word "witness" in the original Greek can best be translated to the word "martyr." A martyr is someone who suffers persecution and death for advocating their beliefs. So, all the followers of Christ are martyrs in persecution or in death. And, right now, I don't think the churches of America are ready for what's to come. Who's going to stand up and be a witness for Christ when real persecution and death comes to our churches? We're not even prepared because no one is really willing to become a true witness of Christ.

The Spirit of Performance

Another sign of the spirit of Babylon in our churches is the spirit of performance. It has been welcomed with open arms. Sadly, we have taken God off the thrones of our hearts and replaced Him with the god of entertainment. Most of the churches are addicted to the outrageous performances that ministers put on and the wildly, out-of-control false prophets--or the wannabe prophets and prophetic ministries. We get bombarded with such high doses of performers that each person has to get more outrageous than the last. We are so concentrated on the worship singers doing vocal backflips and performing for us that it brings in a false spirit of worship.

If you've ever been in a service and noticed that when the spirit of performance comes in, everyone is out of control and some are looking confused, that is the false spirit of worship. When we shut down this spirit for the spirit of worship, a peace and calmness comes over the people. We are losing our positions as worshippers and have become spectators and observers. The earlier church was radical in their worship; it's something that we rarely see anymore due to our 60- to 90-minute service time constraints. They carried a heavy weight of God's glory. The earlier church pressed into God's presence with awe and reverence. Where is that in today's church? We have put our guards down. Now we're seeing the prophetic word of the Apostle Paul manifest: *Men have crept in unawares* (KJV). We now have a false fivefold government controlling the destiny of the churches of Christ in America—and the rest of the world.

13

Dead Man Walking

I've watched a lot of movies where there was a scene with a man on death row. A correction officer handcuffs the person's wrist and ankles, then the scene cuts to them walking down a long hallway with other prisoners shouting out, "Dead man walking! Dead man walking!" How terrifying that has to be, knowing that you're getting ready to die.

Now, imagine how the high priest felt walking down to the Holy of Holies to sprinkle blood onto the mercy seat of the Ark of the Covenant. He had to be so terrified knowing that he was a dead man walking. Yet, before the high priest could go into the Holy of Holies, there were a few things that needed to be done. The high priest couldn't go before the presence of God smelling like human flesh. He had to cover himself with the blood of a pure and innocent lamb. He had to place the blood on his earlobe, big toe and thumbs. The high priest had to become the walking dead.

Man's flesh can't stand in the presence of God or what is called "His glory." See, the priest was foreshadowing Jesus, our high priest who goes before the throne of the Father to sprinkle His blood, which is pure and innocent. Not only that, but what can wash away my sins? Nothing, but the blood of Jesus. The earthly priest was covered by the blood. This blood now allows us to go before the throne of the Father in boldness. In Exodus 33:17-18, 20, Moses asked the Father if He could show him His glory. And the Father said to Moses, *"You cannot see my face, for no man can see me and live."*

The Father only delights in those who become a living sacrifice, holy and acceptable to Him. In today's churches, we don't understand the difference between the anointing and His glory. We tend to say or hear someone say, "The glory of God is in this place." It's not His glory if no one isn't hiding, stumbling or falling flat on their face from the power of it. When the glory of the Father manifests, things fall to the ground, everyone and everything. Scripture says that when the glory of the Lord comes, islands will be moved, mountains will become molehills and the earth will shake. What we see or feel is the anointing that can break all yokes. But human flesh can't stand in the glory of the Father. It's hard to trust someone who says they've been walking with the Lord for most of their lives, yet they are still carnal. You can't walk with God and stay the same.

There was a man named Enoch, the seventh man from Adam, who talked and walked with God and was no more. See, when you die to self, you become no more. No more like you used to be, how you used to act, how you used to talk. Now, you have a limp in your walk. You become one with the Father. The only way you become no more is to become a dead man walking, just like Enoch.

Jesus tells us that, in order to follow and walk with Him, everyone must pick up their cross. In the Greek, the word for "cross" is "stauros," which means "exposure to death." We can't be living sacrifices, waiting on the fire from heaven, if our altars are empty. We've been praying, asking and crying out to God to send the fires from heaven, but no one has lain out at the altar of God. Some of our altars need to be rebuilt, and some haven't had a sacrifice on them in decades. Once we lie out at the altars of God, He then can let His holy fire fall. That's when revival will be birthed and lives will be changed.

14

Empty Altars

The definition of alter is "to change or cause to change in character or composition, typically in a comparatively small, but significant way; make structural change to; tailor (clothing) for a better fit or to conform to fashion." Meanwhile, in the Hebrew tongue, altar is the word "mizbeah." It has a root word that means "to slaughter." And, in the Greek, it is the word "thusiasterion," which means "a place of sacrifice."

In Romans 12:1-2, the Apostle Paul, in a nutshell, is telling us that we have to come to the altar of God: *"I beseech you therefore, brethren, by the mercies of God, that ye present your bodies a living sacrifice, holy, acceptable unto God, which is your reasonable service.* (This can only be done by going to the altar to change, or so that our character can be changed.) *And be not conformed to this world, but be transformed by the renewing of your mind, that ye may prove what is that good, and acceptable and perfect, will of God."* Once we place ourselves on the altar of God, He becomes our tailor, causing a better fit or fashioning us to conform to His will and likeness.

Altars are places where mankind and the holy divine can interact by communication, exchanging the natural for the supernatural. However, altars can be used for good or evil. In 2 Chronicles 28, the king Ahaz was in Damascus. A specific altar caught his eyes. He then sent back the designs of this altar to the high priest in Israel so a replica could be built. Once it was completed, Ahaz made sacrifices to the gods of Damascus to obtain favor or protection from becoming a captive of his enemy. The Bible said it was the end of him, or it was the ruin of him. This king of Israel did evil in the sight of God by using an altar for divination. We have to be *very* careful about coming to the altar of God with the right intent, but a wrong motive, which can ruin us.

Now, looking at the other end of the spectrum, we see the prophetic conflict in 1 Kings 18 between the Prophet Elijah and the prophets of Baal. The prophets of Baal placed their sacrifice on the altar and began to cut themselves. They called upon their god all day, but nothing happened. Elijah then called the people over to him as he repaired or built the altar of God. He then placed his sacrifice on the altar and called on the name of the Lord. Fire came down from heaven before all of the people, and they believed again on the name of the Lord. The event spurned a revival among the people of Israel.

If there's no sacrifice on the altar of God, then the fire of revival can't fall on us. The Father delights in our living sacrifices of repentance and brokenness. If we ever want a move from God that's greater than Azusa Street, the Hebrides Revival, the Welsh Revival, and the Great Awakenings, we have to rebuild our empty altars. We can't avoid repentance and brokenness, and expect the Father to do mighty things. Service after service, we ask Him to come closer, but He can only come so close to the smell of our flesh that's not burning.

If we're going to be really hungry for the Lord, then we need to fill up the altars of the Lord. We need to tell Him, "Here I am, Lord, your living sacrifice! So, let your fire fall down on me."

15

When Idols Fall

In 1 Samuel 5:2, the Word says, *When the Philistine took the ark of God, they brought it into the house of Dagon, and set it by Dagon. And when they of Ashdod arose early on the morrow, behold, Dagon was fallen upon his face to the earth before the ark of the Lord* (KJV).

There's an account in the Bible where the enemies of Israel, the Philistines, defeated them in battle and took the ark of the Lord. They knew all about the Hebrew God that had led them out of Egypt and brought plagues. But they didn't understand the fear and terror of the other surrounding nations. And yet, they took the ark of the Lord into the temple of Dagon. But did they really take the ark, or did God *allow* Himself to be taken?

Dagon was the central god of the Philistines, and this idol was depicted as half fish and half man. Now on the first night, something strange began to happen. Dagon fell to the ground. Can you picture the looks on the faces of those who came to pray and worship in this temple? Dagon is face first on the ground in front of the ark of the Lord. Just imagine the puzzled faces that they must have had. So now, they had to pick up their god and put him back on his feet.

When you have idolatry in your heart, or put anything above God, He will cause it to fall down. He will not allow you and what is unfit to stand in His presence. But we always have a way of picking up our idols again. This is why we need to have Him to create in us a clean heart, and we need to wash our hands before coming into His presence.

After the priest of Dagon got him back on his feet, the Philistines left for the night. The next morning, the worshippers came in to pray and saw Dagon once again on the ground. This time, though, his head had been cut off. Oh, the drama and panic that must have been going on in the camp of the Philistines! At this time, God released a plague in the entire camp of the Philistines until they figured out that it was the ark of the Hebrew God that was causing everything wrong. So, God allowed Himself to be packed up and brought back to the Israelites.

In order to be in the true presence of God, we must get rid of the idols that we have placed on the thrones of our hearts, or God will cause them to crash down into pieces.

Idols aren't the enemy of God, but the enemy of self. These idols will slowly cause us to drift away from God. See, an idol is a substitute for God when we can no longer wait on God. In Exodus, Moses goes up the mountain of Sinai to meet with God. The people of Israel got tired and bored waiting on Moses to return. They even told themselves that Moses had died. One of the dangers in the body of Christ is the spirit of boredom. The spirit of boredom brings with it a spirit of confusion. The people of God get upset and bored with religion's do's and don'ts, and think it's connected to the way and things of God when it's really steeped in men's flesh!

When you have a true encounter with God, there's no turning back—there's no getting bored with God. Looking at this account in Exodus, you'll see that Israel experienced the marvelous works of God time and time again on their behalf, but they got bored of God's works and never desired a relationship with Him. They still had the idols and desires of Egypt on the thrones of their hearts. This only caused them to desire the things that God was doing, like feeding them and keeping them warm at night and cool during the day. But they never desired His presences.

Just like today, we desire His gifts—the things that God has and will do for us—but we no longer long for Him or wait for Him. We've created programs for our services instead of creating an atmosphere for His presence. I pray that God will cause these idols to fall.

16

Preparing for a Visitation

It's going to cost you a lot to prepare for a visitation of the Lord. There are things that you're going to have to strip away from your life. When I was much younger living in Detroit, Michigan, our city was selected by the NFL to host the 2002 Super Bowl XL on November 1, 2000—just two years before the grand opening of the new football stadium that was built. It was a big buzz throughout the city. There was a lot of preparation. Hundreds to thousands of people were coming to visit our city. The plan was put in place immediately on how to beautify our city and make it welcoming. Some buildings were torn down; some were getting new paint jobs; roads, freeways and overpasses were resurfaced. New businesses popped up like hotels, restaurants, and places for outdoor and indoor entertainment. It took a lot, and this took two years for just *one night*.

This reminds me of the story of Esther. The Bible says that Esther spent twelve months preparing for her moment with the King Xerxes (Esther 2:12). But in today's world, everyone is looking for that shortcut to success. Everyone wants to jump out as a finished product and skip over the preparation and process stages that God has ordered. This is why we have a lot of talented and gifted people in the body of Christ who lack character and integrity. Process and preparation produce character and integrity. Most of the people we follow and love are anointed, but they're carrying a sour anointing. They've allowed the flies of Beelzebub to land into the ointment of God's process.

Our contemporary western mindset can't fully understand the protocol of preparation when coming before a king because we're used to presidents and prime ministers. Esther soaked her whole body in myrrh for six months and other wonderful smelling perfumes the other six months. These things were good to the king, but did you know that some of our favorite perfumes could be an *offense* to a king if we were to meet with one in the time of Esther? When we don't follow the protocol of the king, we can be rejected from his presence and palace.

I want to explain prophetically why myrrh had to be used and why we must use it as we prepare for our visitation. Myrrh is a bitter herb, but it releases a sweet scent. The bitterness of repentance and a broken heart release a sweet aroma in the nose of God. Myrrh was used in two holy preparations: for ministry and for worship. We see this happen with the woman with the alabaster box. She anointed the feet of Jesus with myrrh mixed with her tears of repentance. This was not only a natural act of repentance, but it was also a prophetic gesture. Myrrh was used as a thickening agent with frankincense to be burned before God as a holy incense. The myrrh and the woman's tears (frankincense) created a holy incense of prayer for forgiveness, restoration and redemption.

If we're going to have a true visitation of God, we must start preparing with cleansing and purification through repentance. We need to experience *myrrh worship*! The kind of worship that God can smell, not just see and hear. My wife wears a certain perfume that gets me all the time. When I smell it, I want to get closer to her because it's such an inviting smell. I believe God wants to do the same thing. Never underestimate someone's myrrh worship because their moment with the King can change their lives.

17

Daddy, I'm Coming Over

One of the greatest relationships I have is with my dad. I don't care what he's doing. I will call him and say, "I'm coming over" and he'll never tell me I can't come. God, whom I call Daddy, revealed to me one day as I sat with my dad that the relationship that I have with my father is a reflection of the relationship I have with Him. I sat with my dad one evening as he told me things that I never knew about him. My dad showed me another side of him that I'd never seen before. He shared with me his experiences with God through open visions and trances. He shared how my grandmother would know what he was thinking before he would say it. These things drew me closer to my father. I really thought I knew my father, but I found out that I didn't. He is more than just my dad—he has different facets to him.

When it comes to God, He, too, has many facets and many names. The more time you spend with God, the more He'll reveal to you. The more He reveals to you, the more you'll discover that He's more than just God. He is always calling us into intimacy with Him so that we may grow in Him. In order to grow in Him, you must be willing to *come* to Him. In James 4:8, it says, *Come close to God and he will come close to you.* The more I spent time with my father, the closer we grew. I love my father. To this day, he's my best friend and my hero.

God has a divine invitation for you to spend time with Him. God wants to build your faith through the visitation invitation. There are many people who had an encounter with God that changed not only their lives, but their perspective. Let's take John the Revelator, as some may call him, for an example. John always drew so close to Messiah that every time Messiah wanted to reveal deeper revelation, John was always called to be there. John is even known for laying his head on the chest of Messiah. John had the right perspective about Messiah: he wanted to know the heartbeat of Messiah. When you have the heart of God, that's when He'll draw you into intimacy with Him. Here's a few things to know when you draw close to God:

When you draw close to God, you come under His shadow (Psalm 91:1).

When you draw close to God, He becomes a refuge and a fortress (Psalm 91:11).

When you draw close to God, He will cover you with His wings (Psalm 91:4).

When you draw close to God, He becomes your dwelling place (Psalm 91:9).

There's so much that I can say about my father that I can't tell it all. Just sitting with him to hear his stories and wisdom has helped me be a better father to my own children. Sometimes you just have to say, "God! Hey, I'm coming over!"

God is our Father. For some like me, He's my Daddy. You shouldn't have to wait on God to call you to come to Him. He really *desires* for you to come to Him. There is nothing greater than Him hearing His children say, "Daddy, I'm coming over!" With faith of knowing, He'll never say, "I'm busy" or, "No."

Dad, I love you! I'm forever coming over to invade your space.

18

Face to Face

In Exodus 33:11, the Scripture says: *And the Lord spake unto Moses face to face as a man speakth unto his friend* (KJV). This had to be amazing for Moses to speak to the creator of all worlds. In ancient Hebrew culture, the word "face" means "Ayin," which literally means eye to eye. The term "Aph" means nostril to nostril, or breath to breath. That's what I call true intimacy.

Today, we rarely get this kind of intimacy from our romantic partners, family or friends. Social media has connected us, but it has caused us to be detached from reality. Many of us have hundreds to millions of followers or social media friends. Some of us feel a sense that we have a real friend. And that's so far from the truth. Don't get me wrong—social media is good for spreading good news and any other social issues, but we can't mistake this for having a true, intimate relationship. We discover something in the Exodus 33, where God invites everyone to have an intimate relationship with Him.

Exodus 33:7 says, *And Moses took the tabernacle, and pitched it without the camp, afar off from the camp, and called it the tabernacle of the congregation. And it came to pass, that everyone which sought the Lord went out unto the tabernacle of the congregation, which was without the camp* (KJV).

Moses' eyes were opened just a little bit more every time he encountered the presence of the Lord. From the burning bush to the pillar of cloud, the thick cloud on the mountain to the tent of meetings, Moses received revelation upon revelation each time he sought the Lord.

As you read more of Exodus 33, you'll see that when God came down in a cloud, Moses and Joshua would meet with Him. But the strange thing was that Scripture says that the people would stand and watch from their tents as Moses and Joshua walked into the tent of meetings. You have people who will watch you get your blessings, get your breakthrough, get your healing, and watch your encounter with God. Yet, they will never go beyond their dignity in just going to church or having church…whatever that is. Their passion is for church, not for God. Their passion is for the crowds and clowns, not for the cloud.

We have this open-door policy from God to come to Him at any time. He wants a face-to-face relationship, not just a Facebook relationship. You can't have an intimate relationship with anyone on a computer. If you think so, you've been completely deceived. An intimate relationship comes from spending time with a person face to face. All we're doing is collecting people as idols, saying, "Hey, look at me! I have 5,000 friends, but never have a true relationship with any of them." But people should be able to see that you've been with God.

Exodus 34:29 says, *And it came to pass, when Moses came down from Mount Sinai with the two tables of testimony in Moses' hand, when he came down from the mount, that Moses wist not that the skin of his face shone while he talked with him* (KJV).

Moses' face shined with the glory of God, showing that he was *with* God. There have been three other people whose bodies shined. The first two people were Adam and Eve at the time of their creation. Genesis 1:26 says, *And God said, "Let us make man in our image, after our likeness"* (KJV).

The word "image" in the Hebrew is "tselem," which is also used in a shorter form, "tzel," meaning "shadow." We're shadows and a reflection of the Godhead (Father, Son and Holy Spirit). God gave Adam and Eve garments of light, or we can say they had their glorified bodies. This was the only way that they could speak to God face to face because no flesh can stand in the glory of Him. But once they fell, that garment of light, or glory, was lifted off them, and they became naked. So, God had to kill an animal (some say it was a lamb) and gave them the skin (fur or wool) for clothes.

The third person to shine with the glory of God was Jesus at the Mount of Transfiguration.

Matthew 17:2 says, *There he was transfigured before them. His face shone like the sun and his clothes became as white as the light* (KJV).

Just as fast and out of nowhere, the garments of glory appeared upon Jesus and His face was shining. So, we can understand how fast these garments disappeared from Adam and Eve. We will be the last people to put on these garments of glory, as well.

Philippians 3:21 says, *Who will transform our lowly body to be like his glorious body* (KJV).

While thinking of all of this, someone should see that you've been in the presence of God. You should be the shadow that reflects His glory. The longer you spend time with someone, the more you know their heart and mind, the more you know their ways, the more you tend to pick up some of their habits. God is calling us into an intimate relationship with Him. He wants a face-to-face encounter with you. He truly wants us to invade His space.

About the Author

Rahsaan M. Coleman is a prophetic voice to this generation. He's known for his gift of revelation, dream interpretation, prophetic and practical insight, and his passion to see all seek the presence of God. Growing up in a home were no one went to church, Rahsaan's siblings and parents always found him in an upstairs bedroom, talking in front of a window. Little did they know at the time that he wasn't speaking to an imaginary friend—he was having conversations with God.

Under the care of his spiritual father, Bishop David M. Eubanks of New Fellowship C.O.G.I.C, he learned about being radical in his faith to see God do great things. While escorting Bishop Eubanks on an assignment, Rahsaan received a vision into his calling. From that day, his passion has been to walk out his God-given calling. In 2007, Rahsaan's Elijah came to him in the person of Prophet Dennis Hearns of Calvary Cross, where he was trained, cultivated, developed and affirmed as a prophet of God. In 2010, Rahsaan became the youth pastor at New Christian Missionary Baptist Church under the leading of his uncle, Reverend Morris Hampton.

While serving faithfully, Reverend Hampton licensed and ordained Rahsaan as a reverend. Shortly after being ordained, Reverend Hampton had a severe stroke. By request of Reverend Hampton, and the board of deacons, they placed Rahsaan as interim pastor. During his tenure as interim pastor, Holy Spirit spoke to Rahsaan, "The House of Elijah." After a year serving as interim pastor, Rahsaan stepped down to seek God about The House of Elijah.

Within his searching, Holy Spirit showed Rahsaan the work of the prophet and the prophetic to call the people back into relationship with God. Today, Rahsaan has established The House of Elijah's Ministry and The Company of Elijah, where he teaches, trains, disciples and develops those who feel called to the prophetic. He is a bestselling author of the *Invading God's Space* trilogy. Rahsaan has three passions: to seek the presence of God; to help others pursue God; and to train, develop and activate people into their gifts and callings.

www.ingramcontent.com/pod-product-compliance
Lightning Source LLC
Chambersburg PA
CBHW021119020426
42331CB00004B/555